MW01294700

This Notebook Belongs To:

CPSIA information can be obtained
at www.ICGtesting.com
Printed in the USA
BVOW04s1805101217
502450BV00010B/234/P